FOR GARETH

A very special boy.

With my thanks to Kingsley Onye,
for his support and encouragement.

Sheep DON't Go Shopping!

Written by
Pippa Taylor

Illustrated by
Sarah-Leigh Wills

Mum is driving
me to school...

On our way to school Mum says,
'Look out of the window Gareth,
perhaps you will see some sheep!'

So I look and I look... but I can't
see any sheep!

'Never mind,' says Mum. 'Perhaps
the sheep have gone shopping!'

'Oh Mum!' I say...

...'SHEEP DON'T GO SHOPPING!'

We drive a little further along the road and Mum says, 'Look out of the window Gareth, perhaps you will see some cows!'

So I look and I look...but I can't see any cows!

'Never mind,' says Mum. 'Perhaps the cows have gone to the cinema!'

'Oh Mum!' I say...

We drive a little further along the road and Mum says, 'Look out of the window Gareth, perhaps you will see some horses!'

So I look and I look...but I can't see any horses!

'Never mind,' says Mum. 'Perhaps the horses have gone to the hairdressers!'

'Oh Mum!' I say...

...'HORSES DON'T GO TO THE HAIRDRESSERS!'

We drive a little further along the road and Mum says, 'Look out of the window Gareth, perhaps you will see some pigs!'

So I look and I look...but I can't see any pigs!

'Never mind,' says Mum. 'Perhaps the pigs are playing in the playground!'

'Oh Mum!' I say...

...'PIGS DON'T PLAY IN THE PLAYGROUND!'

We drive a little further along the road and Mum says, 'Look out of the window Gareth, perhaps you will see some squirrels!'

So I look and I look...but I can't see any squirrels!

'Never mind,' says Mum. 'Perhaps the squirrels have gone to the swimming pool!'

'Oh Mum!' I say...

We drive a little further along the road and Mum says, 'Look out of the window Gareth, perhaps you will see some ducks!'

So I look and I look...but I can't see any ducks!

'Never mind,' says Mum. 'Perhaps the ducks have gone to the dentist!'

'Oh Mum!' I say...

My Mum is silly sometimes!

www.ingramcontent.com/pod-product-compliance
Lightning Source LLC
LaVergne TN
LVHW072059070426
835508LV00002B/170